TASTY TIFFIN

Also by Archana Doshi

*30 Meal Plans from Archana's Kitchen:
Easy Vegetarian Indian Recipes for Good Health*

TASTY TIFFIN

40+ DELICIOUS AND HEALTHY LUNCH PLANS FOR KIDS

ARCHANA DOSHI

HARPER
NON-FICTION

First published in India by Harper Non-fiction 2024
An imprint of HarperCollins *Publishers*
4th Floor, Tower A, Building No. 10, DLF Cyber City,
DLF Phase II, Gurugram, Haryana – 122002
www.harpercollins.co.in

2 4 6 8 10 9 7 5 3 1

Text and photographs copyright © Archana Doshi 2024

P-ISBN: 978-93-5699-778-3
E-ISBN: 978-93-5699-668-7

The views and opinions expressed in this book are the author's own and the facts are as reported by her, and the publishers are not in any way liable for the same.

This book has been published after all reasonable efforts were taken to make the material error-free. However, the author will not be liable whatsoever for errors and omissions, whether such errors and omissions result from negligence, accident or from any other cause or claims for loss or damages of any kind, including without limitation, indirect or consequential loss or damage arising out of the use, inability to use, or about the reliability, accuracy or sufficiency of the information contained in this book.

All rights reserved. No part of this publication can be reproduced in any manner or stored in a retrieval system, or transmitted, in any form or by any means, electronic, mechanical, photocopying, recording or otherwise, without the prior permission of the publishers or the author.

Archana Doshi asserts the moral right
to be identified as the author of this work.

Typeset in 11/14 Adobe Garamond at
Manipal Technologies Limited, Manipal

Printed and bound at
Replika Press Pvt. Ltd.

This book is produced from independently certified FSC® paper to ensure responsible forest management.

To my mom, who taught me to cook and eat healthy, and packed me the best three-tier lunch boxes ever. The moment I would open it, friends would rush to me, and my lunch box would be empty in minutes.

Contents

How to Pack a School Lunch Box   1

Small Snack Ideas   7

1. Khakhra, Fruit, Cheese Cubes, Walnuts   10
2. Watermelon, Walnuts, Cheese Cubes   10
3. Cookie, Fruit, Walnuts, Cheese Cubes   10
4. Mango, Cheese Cubes, Granola Bar   10

Sandwiches, Pancakes and Waffles   11

5. Choco Chip Pancake, Walnuts, Cheese Cubes   13
6. Multigrain Waffle with Peanut Butter and Marmalade   15
7. Broccoli Paneer Peanut Sandwich, Apples   17
8. Carrot Corn Mayo Sandwich, Fruits   19
9. Cucumber Cheese Sandwich, Walnuts, Banana Almond Date Shake, Cookie/Muffin   21
10. Tofu Veggie Sandwich with Banana Shake   23
11. Grilled Tomato Cheese Pesto Sandwich, Guava, Almonds, Apricots   25

12.	Bagel Pizza and Cookies	27
13.	Bagel Egg Sandwich, Mango Juice	29
14.	Cheesy Spinach Open Toast with Fresh Fruits	31

Quesadilla, Pasta and Noodles — 33

15.	Spinach Corn Quesadilla, Grapes	35
16.	Mushroom Quesadilla, Walnuts, Raisins	37
17.	Desi Masala Pasta, Banana, Boiled Eggs	39
18.	Creamy Tomato Pasta, Stir-Fried Zucchini, Khakhra, Quick Home-made Yogurt Dessert	41
19.	Creamy Mushroom Sauce Pasta, Fresh Fruits	45
20.	Pasta in Spinach Basil Sauce and Apple Banana Almond Date Smoothie	47
21.	Veg Hakka Noodles and Greek Yogurt	50

Indian Tiffin-Style Ideas — 53

22.	Moong Dal Podi Idli, Chutney, Watermelon	55
23.	Oats Rava Dhokla, Cheese Cubes, Almonds	59
24.	Podi Dosa, Date Energy Bar	62
25.	Brown Rice Kozhukattai and Banana	65
26.	Idli Upma, Almonds, Raisins	67
27.	Vegetable Uttapam, Lychee	69
28.	Kuzhi Paniyaram, Banana	71
29.	Palak Paneer Roll, Guava	73
30.	Pav Bhaji	76

31.	Aloo Paratha, Fruit, Raita	78
32.	Rajma Masala, Jeera Pulao	81
33.	Broccoli Peanut Tikki, Fresh Fruits, Greek Yogurt	84

Mixed Rice Ideas   **87**

34.	Vegetable Tomato Rice (Thakkali Sadam) and Curd	89
35.	Cabbage Rice, Stir-Fried Vegetables, Raita	91
36.	Lemon Rice, Curd, Stir-Fried Broccoli	93
37.	Beetroot Rice, Stir-Fried Broccoli, Watermelon Juice	95
38.	Mushroom Biryani, Raita, Papad	98
39.	Green Moong Dal Pulao, Raita, Energy Bar, Makhana	101
40.	Dal Makhani, Jeera Aloo Sabzi, Jeera Rice, Fruits, Nuts	103

Roti Sabzi Ideas   **107**

41.	Broccoli Aloo Sabzi, Phulka, Fruit Salad	109
42.	Methi Bajra Thepla, Channa Masala, Buttermilk	111
43.	Palak Paratha, Chhole Tamatari	115
44.	Paneer Makhani, Pudina Paratha, Raita	119
45.	Quick Gobi Sabzi, Tawa Paratha	123
46.	Matar Paneer, Kala Channa Salad, Paratha	125
47.	Palak Paneer, Tawa Paratha, Cucumber Salad	128

Acknowledgements   130

How to Pack a School Lunch Box

How to Pack a School Lunch Box

Packing a school lunch is a daunting task for most parents and used to be for me too. Trying to balance the nutritional needs of children with the taste and fun element on a daily basis, and preparing food that they will actually eat can be super challenging.

Packing a healthy school lunch box is important for several reasons.

1. First, it provides children with the necessary nutrients and energy to stay focused and engaged in the classroom. A well-balanced lunch should include a variety of fruits and vegetables, whole grains, lean protein and healthy fats.
2. Second, it can help prevent childhood obesity and other health problems associated with a poor diet.
3. Third, it sets a positive example for children, teaching them the importance of making healthy food choices.
4. Finally, it can also help children develop good eating habits that will benefit them in the long term.

Here is how I started thinking about what should go into my child's snack or lunch box. It's simple when you keep these points at the top of your mind. All the ideas in this book are regular, everyday foods we eat at home. They are nothing fancy but just made tasty and appealing using a bento-style packing and, yes, they are healthy too.

Think: Whole Grains for Energy

Carbohydrates are so important for children as they give them the energy needed to put the mind and body to good use in school. It could be in the form of sandwiches, rolls, parathas or rice. Make sure the grains used are whole grains like wheat, rice, oat and millets that give the right nutrition and energy.

Think: Proteins

Proteins are important for brain- and muscle-building for a growing child. Even if it goes in small portions, think cheese cubes, nut butters such as peanut butter and almond butter, eggs in various forms, paneer and yogurt. The protein portion of the meal will keep your child full and help to maintain concentration levels through the afternoon lessons.

Think: Vegetables and Fruit for Vitamins and Fibre

Always add a piece of fresh or dried fruit to your child's lunch box. Children will eat fruit if they are hungry and 'junk' options are unavailable. They bring in the energy and nutrition required for growing children.

And vegetables in any form, whether added as a sabzi or mixed into dosa, paratha or pulao, will still make a small difference in adding the right nutrition.

Think: Water to Drink

Always pack a litre of water. Avoid packaged juices for the lunch box as they come with unhealthy sugars and preservatives. Freeze water bottles the night before for hot summer days. And if packing fresh juices or milkshakes, add a few cubes of ice into the bottle so they stay fresh.

Think: Small Snack

A small snack box apart from the breakfast and lunch box is also required for a child who goes to school for the full day. Think of healthy crackers, wholegrain muffins, low-fat cookies, granola bars and date bars. You can prepare these in bulk and keep them ready for busy school days.

Think: Portion Size and Make It Fun

Consider the portion size appropriate for your child's needs and age, and pack accordingly. Try to make it fun and interactive by cutting fruits and veggies in different shapes; packing a variety of different foods in small bento boxes; or separating them into bite-sized portions.

Small Snack Ideas

Packing seasonal fruits along with nuts and cheese is refreshing for children. Fruits and nuts provide the right amount of nutrition as well. Packing in small amounts breaks the monotony of a meal and gives them an instant burst of energy.

Additions like khakhra and granola bars bring in a tasty bite to the snack box. You can optionally spread some nut butter on the khakhras and sandwich them as a snack.

Packing Tip: Make sure the box is of the right size and the silicone cup holders are compact and fit well. It is also important to place the box horizontally in a lunch carrier. If placed vertically, the chances of food toppling over are high, resulting in a messy lunch box.

Alternatives: You can mix and match seasonal fruits such as grapes and add nuts such as almonds and cashews along with dry fruits such as dates, figs, apricots and raisins.

1

Khakhra, Fruit, Cheese Cubes, Walnuts

2

Watermelon, Walnuts, Cheese Cubes

3

Cookie, Fruit, Walnuts, Cheese Cubes

4

Mango, Cheese Cubes, Granola Bar

Sandwiches, Pancakes and Waffles

5

Choco Chip Pancake, Walnuts, Cheese Cubes

Make mini pancakes and your children will love them. Mini pancakes fit easily into smaller lunch boxes.

Tip: Optionally, slather the pancakes with chocolate spread or drizzle with honey.

Makes: 6 to 8 pancakes

Ingredients

- 1 cup milk
- 1 large egg (optional)
- 1 cup wholewheat flour
- 2 tbsp instant oats
- 2 tbsp jaggery/honey
- 1 tbsp baking powder
- ¼ tsp salt

2 tbsp butter, melted and cooled
½ cup chocolate chips

Method

- In a large mixing bowl, combine all the ingredients except the chocolate chips and whisk to make a smooth pancake batter. Finally, fold in the chocolate chips.
- Preheat a small non-stick pan over low heat. To make mini pancakes, pour a small ladleful of batter into the pan. Cover with a lid and cook for about 2 minutes until lightly browned on the bottom. Flip the pancake and cook until browned on the other side as well for about 2 to 3 minutes. Once done, transfer to a plate. Repeat for remaining pancakes.
- Allow the pancakes to cool and pack into the lunch box.

6

Multigrain Waffle with Peanut Butter and Marmalade

These are the most delicious waffles and make a great snack for kids. Smearing them with nut butter and marmalade gives these waffles that extra-tasty touch.

Makes: 4–6 medium size waffles

Ingredients

1 cup wholewheat flour
½ cup jowar flour
2 tsp baking powder
½ tsp salt
1 pinch ground nutmeg or cinnamon
1 cup milk
1 large egg
Oil, for greasing

Method

- Preheat the waffle iron.
- In a mixing bowl, combine all the ingredients together and whisk until the mixture is smooth.
- Grease waffle iron with oil.
- Pour 2 tbsp of waffle batter into the hot waffle iron and cook until golden brown.
- Once done, allow it to cool before you smear it with nut butter and marmalade. Pack into the lunch box.

7

Broccoli Paneer Peanut Sandwich, Apples

This is a lip-smacking snack of stir-fried broccoli and paneer along with crunchy toasted peanuts, sandwiched between two pillow-soft layers of wholewheat bread. It makes for a delicious high-protein mini meal. If your child is allergic to peanuts, skip them altogether.

Tip: Apples usually stay fresh without discolouration for at least 3 hours. Some children like their apples tossed in lemon and honey, so if your child does too, go ahead and try it out.

Makes: 2 sandwiches

Ingredients

- 1 tsp oil for cooking
- 4 cloves garlic, finely chopped
- 1 cup broccoli, finely chopped
- ½ cup paneer, cut into tiny pieces
- ¼ tsp black pepper powder

2 tbsp roasted peanuts, coarsely pounded
4 slices of wholewheat brown bread
Salt to taste
Butter, for toasting

Method

- Heat oil in a pan over medium heat, add the garlic and sauté for a few seconds. Stir in the broccoli and stir-fry for a couple of minutes until it has softened and feels cooked. Do not overcook as broccoli loses its nutrition when done so.
- Once done, stir in the paneer, salt and pepper and sauté until the ingredients are well combined. Check the taste and adjust seasoning accordingly.
- Turn off the heat, stir in the peanuts and keep aside to cool.
- Preheat the tawa on medium heat.
- On one of the slices place the broccoli, paneer and peanut stuffing and cover it with the other slice to make a sandwich. Smear butter on the top side of the sandwich and place it on tawa. Smear butter on the other side while it is on the tawa.
- Grill on medium heat until the sandwich is golden brown and crisp on both sides.
- Allow it to cool for a couple of minutes, cut into triangular halves and pack.

8

Carrot Corn Mayo Sandwich, Fruits

This sandwich is not only delicious but also provides a good balance of carbohydrates, protein and fibre. It is a perfect meal to pack for lunch as well as enjoy as a quick and healthy snack.

Makes: 2 sandwiches

Ingredients

- 1 medium carrot, grated
- 1 capsicum, finely chopped
- ½ cup sweet corn kernels, boiled
- Salt and pepper, to taste
- 2 tbsp mayonnaise
- 1 tbsp mustard sauce
- 1 tbsp honey
- 4 slices of wholegrain bread
- Butter, for spreading

Method

- In a mixing bowl, combine the carrot, capsicum and corn kernels. Add salt and pepper.
- In a separate bowl, mix together the mayonnaise, mustard sauce and honey to make the dressing.
- Toast the bread slices lightly and butter them. Spread the dressing evenly on each slice of bread.
- Place a generous amount of the vegetable mixture on one slice. Top with the other slice to make the sandwich.
- Cut the sandwiches into halves or quarters and pack.

9

Cucumber Cheese Sandwich, Walnuts, Banana Almond Date Shake, Cookie/Muffin

This sandwich, along with the Banana Almond Date Shake, will ensure your child is energetic throughout the day. The shake is rich in potassium, fibre, healthy fats and protein, making it a great way to fuel the day and keep your child feeling full for hours. Muffins and walnuts can be packed for the small snack box for their mini break.

Makes: 2 sandwiches

Ingredients

- 2 tbsp cream cheese spread
- 1 tbsp mayonnaise
- 1 tsp dried oregano
- 1 tsp crushed black pepper
- 2 sprigs dill leaves, chopped
- 4 slices of wholewheat bread

1 cucumber, sliced
Salt to taste
Butter, for grilling

Method

- In a mixing bowl, add the cream cheese spread along with mayonnaise, dried oregano, black pepper, salt and dill leaves. Mix well to combine.
- Toast the bread slices lightly and butter them. Spread the cream cheese mix evenly on each slice of bread. Arrange the cucumber slices over it. Take another slice of bread, spread some more of the cheese mix and place it over the cucumber.
- Cut the sandwiches into halves or quarters and pack.

Banana Almond Date Shake

Makes: 1 tall glass

Ingredients

1 ripe banana
3–4 Medjool dates, pitted
1 cup milk
2 tbsp almond butter
¼ tsp vanilla extract
1 cup ice cubes

Method

- Add the banana, dates, milk, almond butter and vanilla extract to a blender. Blend on high speed until all the ingredients are well combined and smooth.
- Add the ice cubes and blend again until the shake is thick and creamy. Pour into a leak-proof container and pack.

Khakhra, Fruit, Cheese Cubes, Walnuts (p 10)

Lemon Rice, Curd, Stir-Fried Broccoli (p 93)

Podi Dosa, Date Energy Bar (p 62)

Tofu Veggie Sandwich with Banana Shake (p 23)

Oats Rava Dhokla, Cheese Cubes, Almonds (p 59)

Brown Rice Kozhukattai and Banana (p 65)

Palak Paneer, Tawa Paratha, Cucumber Salad (p 128)

Mango, Cheese Cubes, Granola Bar (p 10)

Bagel Egg Sandwich, Mango Juice, Cheese Cubes (p 29)

Kuzhi Paniyaram, Banana (p 71)

10
Tofu Veggie Sandwich with Banana Shake

Here is a sandwich that is packed with plant-based protein, fibre and other essential nutrients. For the Banana Shake, you can use the same Banana Almond Date Shake recipe (Page 22) and skip the dates if you like. When packing the Banana Shake, use a leak-proof container. Use an insulated lunch box or pack the container with a small ice pack to ensure it stays cold until your child is ready to drink it. You can also add a few ice cubes to the shake for it to stay chilled.

Makes: 2 sandwiches

Ingredients

- ½ cup cabbage, shredded
- 1 carrot, grated
- 1 tomato, finely chopped
- 1 cucumber, finely chopped
- 2 tbsp mayonnaise
- 1 tbsp mustard sauce

1 tbsp honey
½ tsp black pepper powder
150 gm tofu, cut into thin slices
4 slices of wholewheat bread
Salt to taste
Butter, for grilling

Method

- In a mixing bowl, combine the cabbage, carrot, tomato, cucumber, mayonnaise, mustard sauce, honey, salt and pepper. Mix well and keep aside.
- In a pan on medium heat, toast the tofu slices on both sides with 1 tbsp butter until golden brown.
- Toast the bread slices and butter them.
- Take a spoonful of the veggie mayo salad and spread it evenly on the bread. Place the tofu on top of the salad. Top with the other slice of bread to make the sandwich.
- Cut the sandwiches into halves or quarters and pack.

11

Grilled Tomato Cheese Pesto Sandwich, Guava, Almonds, Apricots

A delicious and satisfying lunch option that is perfect for packing in a lunch box. Think slices of ripe, juicy tomato layered with melty cheese and a generous spread of basil pesto, between slices of hearty bread grilled to perfection.

Makes: 1 sandwich

Ingredients

- 2 slices of wholewheat bread
- 1 tbsp prepared pesto
- 4 slices of tomato
- 1 cheese slice
- Salt and pepper to taste
- Butter, for grilling

For the Pesto

200 gm basil leaves
2 tbsp sunflower seeds
6 cloves garlic
¼ cup olive oil
Salt to taste

Method

- To make the pesto, add all the ingredients into a food processor and blend to make a smooth mixture. There is no need to add water as the olive oil will help to blend the ingredients.
- Preheat the tawa on medium heat.
- On one of the bread slices, spread the pesto, place the tomato over it and sprinkle salt and pepper. Next, place the slice of cheese and cover it with the other bread slice to make a sandwich.
- Smear butter on the top side of the sandwich and place it on the tawa. Butter the other side while on the tawa.
- Grill on medium to low heat until the sandwich is golden brown and crisp on both sides.
- Allow it to cool for a couple of minutes, cut into triangular halves and pack.

12

Bagel Pizza and Cookies

This is a great way to use leftover bagels or slices of bread to make a pizza. With olives and sweet corn, it makes for a quick and easy meal that is perfect for a school lunch.

You can also add fruits or nuts to the box. But hey, there are days when we can give this just as a fun treat for lunch.

Makes: 4 open-faced bagel pizzas

Ingredients

    2 plain bagels, sliced in half
    ½ cup pizza or pasta sauce
    ½ cup grated mozzarella cheese
    ¼ cup black olives, sliced
    ¼ cup sweet corn kernels, boiled
    Salt and pepper to taste
    Fresh basil or parsley, chopped, for garnish (optional)

Method

- Preheat your oven to 190°C.
- Place the bagel halves on a baking sheet. Spread a spoonful of the pizza or pasta sauce on each half.
- Sprinkle the mozzarella cheese over the sauce. Add sliced black olives and sweet corn kernels on top of the cheese.
- Season with salt and pepper to taste.
- Bake the bagel pizzas in the oven for 12 to 15 minutes or until the cheese has melted and is bubbling.
- Garnish with fresh basil or parsley, if desired.
- Once cooled, pack into the lunch box.

13

Bagel Egg Sandwich, Mango Juice

A fluffy bagel filled with a high-protein mushroom–egg scramble pairs perfectly with a refreshing Mango Juice that is packed with fruity goodness. It is a breakfast combo that is not only delicious but also energizing, giving young minds the kick-start they need.

Makes: 2 sandwiches

Ingredients

    1 tbsp salted butter
    1 cup button mushrooms, finely chopped
    2 whole eggs
    1 tsp dried oregano
    Small bunch of coriander leaves, chopped
    2 bagels, sliced in half
    2 cheese slices
    Salt and pepper to taste
    Butter, for toasting bagels

Method

- Melt butter in a pan over medium heat. Add the mushrooms and sauté for about 2 minutes, until softened and cooked.
- Add the eggs, oregano, salt and pepper, and scramble the eggs along with the mushrooms.
- Check the salt and pepper and adjust according to taste. Stir in the coriander leaves and keep aside.
- Spread butter over the bagels and toast on a tawa until golden brown and crisp.
- Spoon the mushroom–egg mixture on to one of the slices. Place a cheese slice and top with the other half of the bagel to make a sandwich.
- Cut the sandwiches into halves and pack.

14
Cheesy Spinach Open Toast with Fresh Fruits

In the lunch box, this Cheesy Spinach Open Toast is bursting with the goodness of spinach and melted cheese.

You can add a side of juicy apple slices or sweet oranges. This adds a refreshing touch to balance out the richness of the cheesy spinach toast, making it a perfectly satisfying meal for any young adventurer.

Makes: 2 open toasts

Ingredients

- 2 slices of wholewheat brown bread
- 2 tbsp butter
- 1 tsp oil
- 1 cup spinach leaves, finely chopped
- 2 cloves garlic, finely chopped
- 2 tbsp cheese spread

¼ cup mozzarella cheese, grated
Salt and pepper to taste

Method

- Heat oil in a pan over medium heat, add the garlic and chopped spinach and sauté till they wilt a bit. Stir in the cheese spread along with salt and pepper and keep aside.

- Toast the bread in a bread toaster until lightly brown. Spread butter on the toast, top it with the spinach mixture and sprinkle some cheese on the top.

- Place in an oven toaster grill at 200°C and bake until the cheese melts. Remove from the oven, set aside to cool and pack into the lunch box.

Quesadilla, Pasta and Noodles

Quesadilla, Pasta and Noodles

15
Spinach Corn Quesadilla, Grapes

This is a nutritious meal that is easy to prepare and works perfectly as an easy-to-eat lunch. The quesadillas are made with wholewheat tortillas that are filled with a mixture of sautéed spinach, sweet corn kernels and melted cheese. The spinach adds a healthy dose of vitamins and minerals, while the sweet corn kernels provide a sweet and crunchy texture that complements the savoury flavour of the cheese.

Makes: 8 slices

Ingredients

- 1 cup spinach, chopped
- 1 cup sweet corn, boiled
- 2 tbsp mayonnaise
- 4 wholewheat tortillas
- ½ cup mozzarella cheese, grated
- Salt and pepper to taste
- Olive oil, for cooking

Method

- Heat oil in a saucepan over medium heat, add the spinach and sweet corn and sauté for 2 minutes till the spinach is cooked and all the water evaporates. Turn off the heat.
- Stir in the mayonnaise, salt and pepper and keep aside.
- Preheat a skillet over medium heat; place the tortilla and warm it for a few seconds. Then spoon the spinach-and-corn mixture on to one side of the tortilla, sprinkle cheese and fold the other side on top of the stuffing to create a semicircle.
- Drizzle 1 tsp olive oil and cook on either side of the tortilla till crisp and golden brown. Once done, cut the quesadilla into wedges.
- Allow it to cool before packing into the lunch box.

16

Mushroom Quesadilla, Walnuts, Raisins

The combination of savoury mushrooms and cheese creates a flavour explosion that is sure to satisfy your kids' taste buds. This lunch is easy to cook and can be prepared ahead of time, making it a convenient and delicious option for busy days. Pack it in a lunch box with some dry fruits such as walnuts and raisins, and you have a tasty and nutritious meal that will keep the kids energized and focused throughout the day.

Makes: 8 slices

Ingredients

2 cloves garlic, finely chopped
1 onion, finely chopped
1 cup button mushrooms, chopped
4 wholewheat tortillas
½ cup mozzarella cheese, grated

Small bunch of coriander leaves, finely chopped
Salt and pepper to taste
Olive oil, for cooking

Method

- Heat oil in a saucepan on medium heat. Add the garlic and onion, and sauté until the onion softens and turns slightly brown.
- Next, stir in the mushrooms and sauté for 2 to 3 minutes until they are cooked. Turn off the heat.
- Stir in the chopped coriander leaves, salt and pepper and keep aside.
- Preheat a skillet over medium heat; place the tortilla and warm it for a few seconds. Then spoon the mushroom mixture on to one side of the tortilla, sprinkle cheese and fold the other side over it to create a semicircle.
- Drizzle 1 tsp olive oil and cook on either side till crisp and golden brown. Once done, cut the quesadilla into wedges.
- Allow it to cool before packing into the lunch box.

17

Desi Masala Pasta, Banana, Boiled Eggs

Get ready for a lunch box that is packed with flavour and nutrition! Introducing the Desi Masala Pasta, Banana and Boiled Eggs lunch and snack-box combo—the perfect meal for any adventurous kid!

Bananas are packed with nutrients such as potassium and vitamin C, making them a great addition to any meal. Plus, they are the perfect on-the-go snack for busy kids. The boiled eggs are a protein-packed food, easy to prepare and carry, and will keep your kids fuelled and energized throughout the day.

Makes: 5 servings

Ingredients

300 gm penne pasta
1 tbsp extra virgin olive oil
1 onion, finely chopped
4 cloves garlic, finely chopped
½ green capsicum, finely chopped

4 tomatoes, finely chopped
2 carrots, finely chopped
1 tsp pav bhaji masala
1 tsp garam masala powder
½ tsp red chilli powder
Small bunch of coriander leaves, finely chopped
Salt to taste

Method

- Heat about 3 litres of water and add a little salt. Bring to a boil. Add 3 handfuls or about 300 gm of pasta into the boiling water. Cook the pasta until it has a firm bite, which is an al dente texture. This will take about 7 to 9 minutes.
- Once cooked, drain the water and rinse the pasta in cold running water to stop the cooking process. Drizzle a little oil over the pasta to prevent it from sticking.
- Heat oil in a pan over medium heat. Add the onion, garlic, capsicum and carrots and sauté until the onion and capsicum become tender.
- Add the tomatoes, the pav bhaji masala, garam masala and red chilli powder along with some salt. Stir to combine well.
- Cover the pan, turn the heat to low and cook the masala until the tomatoes become soft and mushy. Once the tomatoes are cooked, stir in the cooked pasta and chopped coriander leaves. Sauté for 3 to 4 minutes; check the salt and adjust accordingly.
- Allow it to cool a bit before you pack it into the lunch box.

Note: You can add a few tablespoons of cream or even cheese spread to make it a little creamy or cheesy.

18

Creamy Tomato Pasta, Stir-Fried Zucchini, Khakhra, Quick Home-made Yogurt Dessert

Your kids get to indulge in a lunch box that is bursting with flavour and texture! This is the Creamy Tomato Pasta, Stir-Fried Zucchini, Khakhra and Quick Home-made Yogurt Dessert combo! It is a lunch and snack-box combo that is both satisfying and exciting, and will leave the child feeling nourished and energized all day long.

Creamy Tomato Pasta

Makes: 5 servings

Ingredients

300 gm pasta
1 tbsp extra virgin olive oil
1 yellow zucchini, cut into slices
1 yellow bell pepper, thinly sliced

¼ cup fresh cream
Salt to taste

For the Tomato Basil Sauce

1 kg tomatoes (red, ripe ones)
1 tbsp extra virgin olive oil
4 cloves garlic, finely chopped
1 onion, finely chopped
4 sprigs basil leaves, roughly torn
1 tsp red chilli flakes
1 tsp dried oregano
Salt and pepper to taste

Method

- Heat about 3 litres of water and add a little salt. Bring to a boil. Add 3 handfuls or about 300 gm of pasta into the boiling water. Cook the pasta until it has a firm bite, which is an al dente texture. This will take about 7 to 9 minutes.

- Strain the water and rinse the cooked pasta in cold water to stop it from cooking further. Drizzle the pasta with olive oil and keep aside.

- The next step is to make the creamy Tomato Basil Sauce. Cut the tomatoes in half and place in a pressure cooker. Allow the tomatoes to pressure cook for just one whistle.

- After the first whistle, release the pressure immediately and allow the tomatoes to cool. Once cooled, drain the water. Remove the skin from the tomatoes and blend the pulp in a mixer-grinder to make a smooth purée. Keep aside.

- Heat olive oil in a saucepan over medium heat. Add the garlic and onion. Sauté the onion until tender. Add the freshly made tomato purée, basil leaves, red chilli flakes, oregano, salt and

pepper and bring the mixture to a brisk boil for 3 to 4 minutes. Keep aside.
- Heat oil in a large pan. Add the zucchini and bell pepper and roast until soft and cooked. Stir in the cooked pasta along with the Tomato Basil Sauce.
- Stir in the cream and sauté on high heat until the pasta gets well coated with the sauce.
- Allow it to cool a bit before you pack it into the lunch box.

Stir-Fried Zucchini

Makes: 2 servings

Ingredients

2 zucchinis, cut into slices
Salt and pepper to taste
½ tsp dried oregano
Olive oil, for cooking

Method

- Heat oil in a wok over medium heat. Add the zucchini slices; sprinkle salt, pepper and oregano, and give it a stir.
- Cook on high heat for about 3 to 4 minutes until the zucchini is cooked.
- Cool and pack into a snack box.

Quick Home-made Yogurt Dessert

This super-easy dessert can be made ahead of time and stored in small jars to last the entire week.

Makes: 2 servings

Ingredients

200 gm hung curd or Greek yogurt
4 tbsp powdered sugar
½ tsp vanilla extract
½ cup chopped fruits such as grapes, mangoes, oranges
2 biscuits, crushed into a coarse powder (optional)

Method

- Whisk the hung curd along with powdered sugar and vanilla extract.
- Layer a container or jar with dollops of this yogurt and seasonal fruits.
- You can also top it with a biscuit crumble or nuts.

19

Creamy Mushroom Sauce Pasta, Fresh Fruits

In the lunch box, Creamy Mushroom Sauce Pasta is absolutely cozy and comforting. Pack it along with a mix of cut seasonal fruits such as juicy strawberries, grapes, pineapples, bananas, apples and kiwis. This is a simple, satisfying duo, offering a taste of home and a burst of freshness for a delicious midday break.

Makes: 4 servings

Ingredients

    300 gm durum wheat pasta
    250 gm button mushrooms, roughly chopped
    6 cloves garlic, finely chopped
    ½ tsp black pepper powder
    ½ tsp cumin powder, to taste
    ¼ cup peppery cheese spread
    1 cup milk

A small bunch of coriander leaves, finely chopped
Salt to taste

Method

- Start by boiling the water along with a little salt. Once the water comes to a boil, add the pasta and cook until it has a firm bite, which is an al dente texture.
- Strain the water from the cooked pasta and rinse it under cold water. Drain all the water and drizzle olive oil over the pasta so it does not stick to each other.
- To make the sauce, heat oil in a saucepan, add garlic and mushroom and sauté for about 10 minutes, till the mushroom releases all moisture and becomes dry.
- Once cool, add the mushroom, milk, cheese spread, salt, cumin, pepper and blend to make a smooth purée.
- Now into a pan, add a little more olive oil, the cooked pasta and the mushroom sauce. Gently toss the pasta till it is evenly coated with the sauce and bring it to a brisk boil for a couple of minutes. Turn off the heat and stir in the coriander leaves.
- Once cooled, pack the pasta into the lunch box along with a bowl of mixed cut fruits.

20

Pasta in Spinach Basil Sauce and Apple Banana Almond Date Smoothie

Here is a delicious pasta swirled in a vibrant spinach basil sauce that is filled with nutrition, freshness and fun. Pack it along with an Apple Banana Almond Date Smoothie, a nutritious blend brimming with energy and sweetness. Together, they create a nourishing, flavourful and balanced meal, ready to fuel young minds and bodies for the adventures of the day ahead.

Makes: 4 servings

Ingredients

For the Pasta

    1 tsp extra virgin olive oil
    300 gm pasta
    1 tbsp dried mixed herbs
    1 tbsp salt

For the Spinach Basil Sauce

1 tsp extra virgin olive oil
4 cloves garlic, finely chopped
3 cups spinach, chopped
1 tsp cumin powder
1 cup milk
2 tbsp cream cheese
A few sprigs of basil leaves
1 tsp crushed black pepper
Salt to taste

Method

- Cook the pasta in water along with a little salt until it is has a firm bite, which is an al dente texture. Once it is cooked, rinse it under cold water and drizzle a little oil over the pasta to prevent it from sticking to each other.
- Heat olive oil in a pan. Once the oil is hot, add the finely chopped garlic and sauté for a few seconds. Then, add the chopped spinach, salt to taste, pepper powder and cumin powder.
- Let it cook till the spinach wilts or becomes soft. Once done, turn off the heat and keep it aside to cool.
- Now, add the cooked spinach, milk, basil leaves, cream cheese in a blender and blend to make a smooth purée. Keep it aside.
- Next, heat olive oil in a heavy bottomed pan. Once the oil is hot, add the cooked pasta, mixed herbs, spinach basil purée into the pan and mix them well. Stir fry on high heat for 3 to 4 minutes until the pasta gets well coated and has a nice creamy consistency. Once done, turn off the heat.
- Allow it to cool and pack into the lunch box.

For the Smoothie

Makes: 2 cups

1 apple, peeled and diced
1 small banana, peeled and diced
3 dates, pitted
10 whole almonds, soaked for 1 hour
1½ cups chilled milk

Method

- Blend the apple, dates, banana and almonds with just half the milk, until smooth.
- Add the remaining milk and blend again to combine well. Open the jar and pour the smoothie into a leak-proof bottle for kids to take to school.

21

Veg Hakka Noodles and Greek Yogurt

A wonderul recipe that is a tangle of colourful veggies mixed with slurp-worthy noodles, offering a tasty twist on a classic kids' favourite dish. Pack this box along with a bowl of fruits or a creamy cup of fruity Greek yogurt, adding a touch of tangy goodness to the meal. This is a simple and satisfying combo that offers the perfect fuel to power children through their day.

Makes: 4 servings

Ingredients

- 150 gm pack of Hakka noodles
- 2 onions, thinly sliced
- 1-inch ginger, finely chopped
- 1 carrot, thinly sliced
- 1 capsicum, thinly sliced
- 1 cup cabbage, thinly sliced
- ½ cup green beans, thinly sliced

4 sprigs of spring onion, chopped
½ tsp black pepper powder
½ tsp soy sauce
1 tsp red chilli sauce
½ tsp chilli vinegar
1 tbsp oil
Salt to taste

Method

- Add 1 litre of water in a pan and bring it to a boil. Add the noodles to the boiling water and cook them until just about cooked; it should have a firm bite, which is an al dente texture.
- Cool the noodles immediately by running them under cold water. This stops the cooking process and prevents the noodles from getting too soft and soggy. Add a tablespoon of oil to the cooled noodles to prevent sticking and keep aside.
- Heat oil in a large frying pan on high heat. Once the oil is hot, add the sliced onions and ginger and sauté until the onions have softened.
- Once done, add the capsicum, carrots, beans, cabbage, spring onions, salt to taste and pepper powder and sauté on high heat until the vegetables have a cooked and crisp texture. Stirring on high heat cooks the vegetables faster and also helps them retain colour and a subtle crispness.
- You can even cover the vegetables and cook them for 3 minutes.
- Once the vegetables are cooked yet firm, stir in the soy sauce, chilli sauce and chilli vinegar and stir fry for 2 minutes.
- Once done, stir in the cooked noodles and mix well to combine. Turn off the heat and transfer noodles to a serving bowl. Allow the noodles to cool before packing into the lunch box.

Indian Tiffin-Style Ideas

Indian Tiffin-Style Ideas

Watermelon, Walnuts, Cheese Cubes (p 10)

Choco Chip Pancake, Walnuts, Cheese Cubes (p 13)

Broccoli Paneer Peanut Sandwich, Apples (p 17)

Vegetable Uttapam, Lychee (p 69)

Idli Upma, Almonds, Raisins (p 67)

Multigrain Waffle with Peanut Butter and Marmalade (p 15)

Vegetable Tomato Rice (Thakkali Sadam) and Curd (p 89)

Quick Gobi Sabzi, Tawa Paratha (p 123)

Broccoli Paneer Peanut Sandwich, Apples (p 17)

Pav Bhaji (p 76)

22

Moong Dal Podi Idli, Chutney, Watermelon

Kids will simply love these soft mini Moong Dal Podi Idlis along with a juicy fruit for that extra yum! The watermelon chunks bring a splash of freshness to the lunch box, making the kids feel satiated. You can leave out the Chutney or add just a tablespoon of it for added taste.

Makes: 40 mini idlis

Ingredients

For the Moong Dal Idli

- 1 cup yellow moong dal (split)
- 1 tsp methi seeds
- 1 cup idli rice
- Salt to taste
- Ghee, for greasing

For the Thengai Milagai Podi

Makes: 2 cups

¼ cup channa dal
¼ cup white urad dal (split)
2 tbsp sesame seeds
5–6 dry red chillies
1 cup desiccated coconut
½ tsp asafoetida
30 gm tamarind
Salt to taste
½ tsp Kashmiri red chilli powder

For the Seasoning

2 tbsp ghee
1 tsp mustard seeds
1 tsp black urad dal (split)
2 sprigs curry leaves

Method

- The first step is to make the Moong Dal Idli batter.
- Soak the moong dal and methi seeds together in a bowl of water and soak the rice separately in another bowl of water for three hours.
- After three hours, blend the moong dal and methi seeds in a mixer-grinder to make a smooth batter along with a little water and pour into a large bowl.
- Place the rice in the same blender and blend to make a smooth, thick batter. Pour the rice batter into the moong dal batter. Add salt and mix well to combine. Cover the bowl and allow it to ferment for 8 hours.

- After 8 hours, you will notice air pockets in the batter. Gently mix and keep aside.
- Grease a mini idli mould with ghee and spoon the batter into each cavity. Steam the Moong Dal Idlis for 15 minutes. Once done, remove from the pan and place in a serving bowl, cover and keep aside. You can get 40 mini idlis with this recipe.
- Next, to make the Thengai Milagai Podi, we will roast all the ingredients separately on medium heat so that the dals and other ingredients do not burn.
- Heat a pan on medium heat and first roast the channa dal until it turns golden brown. Keep in a bowl and allow it to cool.
- In the same pan, roast the urad dal till golden brown. Keep in a bowl and allow it to cool.
- Add the sesame seeds and roast for a few seconds until they begin to pop. Keep in a bowl and set aside.
- Finally, roast the desiccated coconut till it starts to turn golden brown. Do not brown it too much. Keep stirring in between. Place in a bowl and allow it to cool.
- Once the dals and all the other ingredients have cooled, add them to a mixer-grinder along with asafoetida and tamarind, and grind. Add salt and chilli powder and grind again to get a coarse powder.
- Transfer the Thengai Milagai Podi to a bottle. You can store this in the refrigerator for a couple of months.
- The final step is to make the Moong Dal Podi Idli. Heat ghee in a frying pan over medium heat. Add the mustard seeds and black urad dal. Allow the mustard seeds to crackle and the dal to become crisp and golden brown.

- Add the curry leaves and 2 to 3 tbsp of the Thengai Milagai Podi. Add the steamed idlis to the pan and toss until all the idlis are well coated with the Thengai Milagai Podi. Turn off the heat and allow them to cool.
- Pack into the lunch box as it is or along with a coconut chutney and fruit slices.

23

Oats Rava Dhokla, Cheese Cubes, Almonds

Oats Rava Dhoklas are fluffy and nutritious, topped with a zesty tadka and served with a side of crunchy almonds for a power-packed punch. And there's more—the fun cheesy cubes make it a balanced meal that will keep your kid energized and smiling all day long!

Makes: 15–20 dhokla pieces

Ingredients

1 cup sooji (rava), roasted
½ cup instant oats
½ cup plain curd/yogurt
1 tsp Eno fruit salt
Salt to taste
Red chilli powder, for sprinkling

For the Seasoning

1 tbsp oil, plus extra oil for greasing
½ tsp mustard seeds
1 tsp sesame seeds
¼ tsp asafoetida
2 green chillies, slit
5 curry leaves

For the Garnish

Handful of coriander leaves, finely chopped
Fresh coconut, grated

Method

- In a mixing bowl, add the roasted sooji, instant oats, yogurt and salt to taste. Add water, a little at a time, and stir to make a thick batter.
- Allow the batter to rest for 5 minutes and add Eno fruit salt. Stir well to combine.
- Prepare the dhokla steamer with water and preheat it on medium heat. Grease the dhokla pans with oil.
- Pour the dhokla batter into the greased dhokla pans. Sprinkle a little red chilli powder over the dhokla and place in the steamer.
- Cover the steamer and let it steam for about 10 to 15 minutes until a tester, such as a butter knife, comes out clean when inserted. Once done, turn off the heat. Remove the stand from the steamer and allow it to rest for a couple of minutes.
- Cut the dhokla into squares or diamonds and arrange them on a serving platter. Keep aside.

- Into a preheated pan over medium heat add oil. Once the oil is hot, add the mustard seeds, sesame seeds and asafoetida. Allow the seeds to crackle.
- Add the green chillies and curry leaves. Stir for a few seconds and turn off the heat. Spread the seasoning over the dhokla. Garnish with the coriander leaves and grated coconut.
- Once cooled, pack the dhokla into the lunch box along with nuts and cheese cubes or even a fresh fruit.

24

Podi Dosa, Date Energy Bar

This scrumptious Podi Dosa makes for a great lunch when made with ghee and sprinkled with the irresistible Thengai Milagai Podi (Page 56). Pack it along with a wholesome granola bar loaded with dry fruits, nuts and grains for a delightful crunch. It is a meal that is not only delicious but also keeps the child powered up throughout the day.

Tip: Use a dosa batter you make at home or even the Moong Dal Batter we used to make idlis (Page 55). You can make energy bars easily at home and stock them for weeks or even buy them from stores.

Makes: 4 dosas

Ingredients

1 cup Moong Dal batter (Page 55)
Thengai Milagai Podi (Page 56)
Ghee, for cooking

Method

- Heat a skillet or dosa tawa on medium heat. Pour a ladleful of the dosa batter on the skillet and spread in a circular motion to make a thin dosa.

- Drizzle 1 tsp ghee around the dosa and cook until it is golden brown and crisp. Once done, sprinkle the podi over the dosa and fold in half.

- Repeat the process for the remaining dosas. To pack into a lunch box, cut the dosa into triangles. Allow it to cool and pack along with energy bars.

Date Energy Bar

Makes: 20–25 bars

Ingredients

500 gm dates, pitted
½ cup cocoa powder
¼ cup soy granules
½ cup instant oats
1 cup whole almonds, powdered
½ cup flax seeds, powdered
¼ cup honey

Method

- Grind the dates in a food processor until you get a dough-like consistency. Add the remaining ingredients into the processor and blend well.

- Divide the date dough into lemon-sized balls, each weighing about 50 gm.

- Grease a cookie cutter and place it on a flat surface. Press a date-dough ball uniformly into the cutter. Lift the cutter and press the date bar out.
- These are now ready to be packed as a snack for kids. Store in airtight containers.

25
Brown Rice Kozhukattai and Banana

Brown Rice Kozhukattai are soft dumplings crafted with care that make for a healthy twist on tradition. Paired with a ripe banana for a natural touch of sweetness, this is a combo that will satisfy your kids' taste buds and keep them fuelled for fun. Nourishing and delicious, this is just what they need to conquer the school day!

Makes: 12–15 Kozhukattai dumplings

Ingredients

- 2 tbsp oil
- 1 cup brown rice rava or regular rice rava
- 1 tsp salt
- 1 cup coconut, freshly grated
- 1 tsp mustard seeds
- 2 tbsp white urad dal (split)
- 3 dry red chillies
- 3–4 curry leaves

Method

- First we have to cook the brown rice rava like an upma. My preferred method to cook this is in a pressure cooker. You can also use a saucepan but it will take a little longer to cook.

- Heat 1 tsp oil in the pressure cooker. Add the brown rice rava, salt and 1½ cups of water. Close the pressure cooker lid and cook the brown rice rava for a couple of whistles, then turn off the heat. Allow the pressure to release naturally.

- Transfer the cooked brown rice rava to a large bowl. Stir in the coconut and check the salt level.

- Steam the brown rice rava along with the coconut. This process of double cooking makes the brown rice rava fluffy and soft. Prepare a steamer and line the steamer plates with oil.

- Shape the coconut–rice rava mixture into oval-shaped dumplings of about 1-inch diameter and place on the steamer plate. Steam for about 10 minutes on high heat and turn off the heat. Remove dumplings from the steamer and keep aside.

- The next step is to season. Heat 1 tbsp of oil in a wok or a heavy-bottomed pan. Add mustard seeds and urad dal and allow them to crackle. Add red chillies and curry leaves and stir until the red chillies are well roasted.

- Add the steamed Kozhukattai to the above seasoning and stir-fry for about 3 to 4 minutes. Remove from heat and allow it to cool before packing it into the lunch box.

26

Idli Upma, Almonds, Raisins

This fluffy Idli Upma is a delightful savoury treat. Pack this along with a handful of almonds for a powerful brain boost. For a touch of natural sweetness, pack some raisins that add a pop of flavour. It's a trio of taste and energy, specially crafted to keep young minds sharp and active all day long.

Tip: Use leftover idlis; dice them up and make this delicious upma. You can use the same Moong Dal Idli Batter mentioned earlier (Page 55) to make the idlis as well.

Makes: 4 servings

Ingredients

- 1 tbsp sesame oil/sunflower oil
- ½ tsp mustard seeds
- 1 tsp white urad dal (split)
- 1 large onion, finely chopped
- 1-inch ginger, finely chopped

3 green chillies, finely chopped
6 curry leaves, finely chopped
1 carrot, finely chopped
1 capsicum, finely chopped
½ cup beans, finely chopped
½ tsp turmeric powder
10 idlis, cut into small pieces
Small bunch of coriander/mint leaves, finely chopped
Salt to taste

Method

- Heat oil in a heavy-bottomed pan over medium heat. Add the mustard seeds and allow them to crackle for a few seconds. Then add the urad dal and roast until it turns light brown and crisp.
- Add the chopped onion, ginger, green chillies and curry leaves. Sauté on medium heat until the onion is translucent. Add the carrot, capsicum and beans; sprinkle salt and roast the vegetables on medium heat.
- You can optionally sprinkle some water, cover the pan and steam-cook the vegetables. Once tender, add the turmeric powder, the idli pieces and some salt to taste.
- Sprinkle a little water so that the idlis don't get too dry. You want them to be moist and flavourful.
- Stir all the ingredients well. Turn the heat to low, cover the pan and allow the Idli Upma to simmer for about 3 to 4 minutes.
- Finally, add the mint/coriander leaves and stir. Turn off the heat and allow it to cool before packing.

27

Vegetable Uttapam, Lychee

This Vegetable Uttapam makes the lunch box a colourful medley of flavours hidden inside fluffy pancakes. Pairing it with the sweetness of lychee or any other seasonal fruit adds a dose of fun and nutrition to your kids' school day.

Makes: 10–12 mini uttapams

Ingredients

2 small carrots, grated
1 onion, finely chopped
2 green chillies, finely chopped
Small bunch of coriander/mint leaves, finely chopped
2 cups dosa batter, as needed
Salt to taste
Oil, for cooking

Note: You can use regular idli batter or the Moong Dal Idli batter as described earlier (Page 55).

Method

- Combine the carrots, onion, green chillies, coriander/mint leaves and salt in a mixing bowl. Keep aside.
- Heat a skillet on medium-high heat. Season it with oil if you are using an iron skillet.
- Check if the skillet is hot: you will know it's ready when you sprinkle some water and it sizzles.
- Pour a ladleful of the dosa batter onto the skillet and give it a light swirl to spread it. It should be like a thick pancake.
- Sprinkle a generous amount of the veggie mixture over the spread batter. Drizzle some oil around the uttapam and cover if you have a lid. You can also let it cook in the open skillet on low to medium heat.
- Once you notice that the top is lightly steamed and the batter is no longer raw, flip the uttapam to cook the other side (with the veggies facing down).
- Turn the heat to medium-high, so the vegetables cook fast. After about 30 to 40 seconds, flip again and the uttapam will be ready. Allow it to cool before you pack into the lunch box.

28

Kuzhi Paniyaram, Banana

Kuzhi Paniyarams are bite-sized wonders that are crispy outside and soft inside—a mini feast of flavours. Paired with a ripe banana that not only offers natural sweetness but also a dose of energy, it is a perfectly balanced meal, keeping the child fuelled and ready for a day of learning and play.

Makes: 25–30 paniyarams

Ingredients

- ¼ tsp mustard seeds
- 1 sprig of curry leaves, finely chopped
- 1 onion, finely chopped
- 2 cups ragi dosa batter (or regular dosa batter)
- 2 tbsp fresh coconut, grated
- ¼ cup carrot, grated
- 1 green chilli, finely chopped
- Salt to taste
- Oil, for cooking

Method

- Heat oil in a small pan over medium heat; add the mustard seeds and curry leaves and cook till they crackle. Add the chopped onion and sauté until tender.
- In a mixing bowl, add the dosa batter, coconut, carrot, green chilli followed by the prepared onion mixture. Add salt to taste and stir well to combine.
- Preheat a paniyaram pan and add ½ tsp oil into each of the cavities. Spoon the dosa batter into the greased cavities; place the pan on medium heat and cover with a lid.
- After 3 to 4 minutes of steaming, you will notice that the tops of the paniyarams are cooked and steamed.
- At this point, turn over each paniyaram to cook the other side. This time around do not cover with a lid. Cook on medium-low heat until the bottom of each paniyaram is browned and crisp.
- Once done, transfer the paniyarams to a bowl and allow them to cool. Proceed the same way with the remaining batter. Once cooled, pack into the lunch box along with fruits and nuts of your choice.

29

Palak Paneer Roll, Guava

This Palak Paneer Roll is a delightful blend of paneer bhurji and nutritious spinach paratha, making it absolutely delicious. Packing it along with the fresh and tropical goodness of guava makes the lunch box juicy and refreshing. Filled with vitamins and yumminess, this combo fuels both body and mind.

Makes: 4 rolls

Ingredients

For the Palak Paratha

½ cup spinach leaves
1 green chilli, finely chopped
1 cup wholewheat flour
½ tsp cumin powder
Salt to taste
1 tsp oil, for kneading
Oil/ghee, for cooking

For the Paneer Bhurji Filling

150 gm paneer, crumbled
1 onion, thinly sliced
1 green chilli, finely chopped (optional)
¼ tsp red chilli powder
½ tsp garam masala powder
¼ tsp turmeric powder
Salt to taste
Small bunch of coriander leaves, finely chopped

For the Roll

Cream cheese spread
Mustard sauce

Method

- Purée the spinach along with the green chilli and keep aside. In a mixing bowl, add the wheat flour, palak purée, cumin powder and salt, and knead to make a smooth dough, adding water if required.
- Finally, add 1 tsp oil and knead well to make a soft Palak Paratha dough. Divide the dough into 4 portions.
- Heat a skillet over medium heat to make the Palak Parathas. Dust the dough with flour and roll to make a large 8-inch circle.
- Cook the Palak Paratha on the hot skillet. Drizzle ghee or oil over the paratha and cook on both sides until cooked through.

You will see light brown spots on both sides. Prepare all the parathas in a similar way and stack them.
- The next step is to make the Paneer Bhurji. Combine all the ingredients in a mixing bowl. Check the salt and spices and adjust to suit your taste.
- To make the wrap, spread a spoonful of cream cheese and mustard sauce on each paratha. Spoon the Paneer Bhurji mixture into the paratha. Roll into a wrap and pack into the lunch box.

30

Pav Bhaji

Pav Bhaji, a medley of mashed veggies bursting with taste and colour, turns lunchtime into a tasty break. Pack this along with a bowl of fruits or even yogurt for a light and fresh touch.

Makes: 4 servings

Ingredients

    6 pav buns
    Salted butter, for toasting

For the Bhaji

    1 tbsp oil
    1 onion, finely chopped
    4 cloves garlic, finely chopped
    1 capsicum, finely chopped
    2 large potatoes, peeled and diced
    1 carrot, diced
    ½ cup cabbage, chopped

½ cup green peas, steamed
1 cup tomato purée
2 tbsp pav bhaji masala
1 tbsp chaat masala powder
2 tbsp butter
1 tbsp lemon juice
Small bunch of coriander leaves, finely chopped
Salt to taste

Method

- Heat 1 tbsp oil in a pressure cooker over medium heat. Add the onion, garlic and capsicum. Sauté on low heat until the onion and capsicum are tender. Add all the vegetables, tomato purée, pav bhaji masala, chaat masala and salt. Add ½ cup water and pressure cook for 4 to 5 whistles, then turn off the heat.
- Allow the pressure to release naturally. Open the lid and mash all the vegetables until you get a smooth texture. Check the taste, add the butter, squeeze in the lemon juice and stir in the coriander leaves. The bhaji is ready.
- Slice the pav buns in half, smear with butter and toast on a skillet until lightly crisp on both sides. Once cooled, pack into the lunch box.

31

Aloo Paratha, Fruit, Raita

This soft and fluffy Aloo Paratha is stuffed with spiced potatoes and cooked to golden perfection. It makes for a delectable and easy-to-eat lunch and, when packed with a juicy fruit and Raita, becomes even more delicious and nourishing.

Tip: Cook the potato masala filling and knead the paratha dough the previous evening, and making the paratha the next morning will be a breeze.

Makes: 8–10 parathas

Ingredients

For the Paratha Dough

    2 cups wholewheat flour
    1 tsp salt
    Water, for kneading
    Ghee, for cooking

For the Filling

4 potatoes, boiled and mashed
2 onions, finely chopped
1-inch ginger, finely chopped
2 green chillies, finely chopped
¼ cup coriander leaves, finely chopped
1 tsp cumin powder
1 tsp coriander powder
1 tsp dry mango (amchur) powder
1 tsp garam masala powder
1 tsp red chilli powder
Salt to taste

Method

- In a large bowl, add 2 cups of wholewheat flour and salt. Use your fingers and mix the salt into the flour. Add water, a little at a time, and knead to make a soft, pliable paratha dough. Knead for a couple of minutes until the dough is smooth and elastic. Use the fold, press and knead motion to make the dough smooth.

- Divide the dough into 8 to 10 equal portions. Cover and allow it to rest while you get the filling ready.

- In a mixing bowl, mash the potatoes into a coarse, lump-free texture with your fingers or a fork.

- Add the onions, ginger, green chillies, coriander leaves, salt to taste, cumin powder, coriander powder, dry mango powder, garam masala and, finally, if you want it extra spicy, the red chilli powder. Using your fingers again, mix all the ingredients into the mashed potatoes until well combined.

- Divide this Aloo Paratha filling into 8 to 10 equal portions. This process of dividing and keeping the portions of dough and filling ready helps you gauge the number of parathas you can make and adjust if you need more or less of the filling.

- Lightly dust each paratha dough portion with wholewheat flour, flatten it with your fingers and place it on a flat surface. Roll it out thin, to approximately 3 inches in diameter.
- Take a portion of the filling and place it in the centre. Next, gather the sides of the paratha dough and bring them together. Remove the little excess dough which pops out when you bring the edges together. Press the stuffed dough ball gently to flatten it.
- Dust the stuffed dough ball with some flour and roll it gently, applying very little pressure. Roll it to the desired thickness and proceed in the same way with the remaining portions of paratha dough and filling.
- Preheat a skillet on medium heat and place the Aloo Paratha on it. Allow it to cook on medium heat for about 30 to 45 seconds and flip it over.
- At this stage, add 1 tsp of ghee (or oil) and spread it on the paratha. Flip again, so the oiled side can cook on the skillet. Spread a little more ghee and keep pressing the paratha while on the skillet to cook it evenly from within.
- Do the flipping over process a couple of times until both sides get evenly cooked, browned and crisp. Make sure you cook on medium heat as it allows the Aloo Paratha to become crisp on the outside.
- Once the Aloo Paratha is cooked, transfer to a plate. Allow it to cool, cut it into triangles and pack into the lunch box.

Raita

In a mixing bowl, add the chopped tomatoes, cucumber, cumin powder and salt. Stir well to combine. Make this the previous day and refrigerate it. Pour the chilled Raita into a leak-proof box for lunch.

32

Rajma Masala, Jeera Pulao

This lunch box features the delightful Indian feast of Rajma Masala, rich and aromatic, with tender kidney beans simmered in a flavourful blend of spices. Pack it along with Jeera Pulao that makes a perfect side for soaking up the hearty flavours of the rajma. It's a simple and delicious combo that's sure to make lunchtime a hit!

Makes: 4 servings

Ingredients

For the Rajma Masala

2 cups rajma, soaked for 8 hours
1 tsp oil
1 onion, roughly chopped
1-inch ginger, finely chopped
1 tomato, finely chopped or puréed
¼ tsp turmeric powder
1 tsp cumin powder
1 tsp Kashmiri red chilli powder

1 tsp garam masala powder
1 bay leaf
1-inch cinnamon stick, broken
A small bunch of coriander leaves, chopped
Salt to taste

Method

- Heat a teaspoon of oil on medium heat in the pressure cooker pan; add the onion and ginger and sauté for 3 to 4 minutes until the onion softens and turns light golden.
- Stir in the tomatoes, bay leaf, cinnamon stick, turmeric powder, cumin powder, red chilli powder, garam masala powder and salt to taste.
- Sauté for another couple of minutes until the tomatoes become soft and mushy.
- Once soft, add the soaked rajma along with its water. Add any additional water if required. There should be enough water such that the water level is at least 2 inches above the rajma.
- Cover the pressure cooker, place the weight on and cook on low to medium heat for about 40 minutes.
- Once done, turn off the heat and allow the pressure cooker to rest and release its pressure naturally. The rajma will continue to cook as long as there is pressure inside the cooker.
- Once the pressure has released, open the cooker. The rajma should now be cooked completely. If you press the rajma between your fingers it will get mashed easily.
- If you find the rajma is still firm, you need to cook it for a little longer. This happens when your rajma bean has aged and hence takes a longer time to cook.

- Once the Rajma Masala is cooked, check the salt and spice levels and adjust to suit your taste.
- Stir in the chopped coriander leaves and add to the lunch box.

For the Jeera Rice

1 cup rice
2 tsp cumin seeds
4 cardamom pods
4 cloves
2 tbsp ghee
2 green chillies, slit
Salt to taste

Method

- Place the washed rice in the pressure cooker, add salt, green chillies and two cups of water.
- Cover the pressure cooker and cook for 2 whistles on high heat. Turn the heat to low and simmer for 3 to 4 minutes and turn off the heat. Allow the pressure to release naturally.
- The rice should rest for 10 minutes before you can open the cooker.
- Heat ghee in a small pan over medium heat. Add the cumin seeds, cardamom pods and cloves. Once they start crackling and you can smell the roasted aromas, turn off the heat.
- Pour the roasted spices into the cooked rice and using a slotted spoon, stir the rice gently and fluff it up. Add to the lunch box.

33

Broccoli Peanut Tikki, Fresh Fruits, Greek Yogurt

This crunchy Broccoli Peanut Tikki, packed with veggie goodness and nutty flavour, makes a great snack that is both delicious and nutritious. You can additionally pair it with a toasted pav or a dinner roll to add in some carbs.

Packing this along with fresh fruits and a creamy Greek yogurt adds a protein-packed touch, perfect for dipping fruits or enjoying on its own for a satisfying and wholesome dessert. It's a simple yet satisfying meal, filled with flavour and goodness, ready to fuel the little ones through their day of fun and learning.

Makes: 8 tikkis

Ingredients

- ½ tsp extra virgin olive oil
- 1 cup broccoli, grated
- 3 potatoes, boiled and mashed

½ cup roasted peanuts, coarsely crushed
2 tbsp instant oats, powdered
2 green chillies, finely chopped
2 cloves garlic, finely chopped
¼ tsp garam masala powder
1 tsp chaat masala powder
Salt to taste

Method

- Into a mixer-grinder, add the instant oats and blend into a powder and keep aside. Pound the shelled, roasted peanuts in a mortar and pestle and keep aside.

- Into a large mixing bowl, add the broccoli, boiled and mashed potatoes, green chillies, garlic, powdered oats, chaat masala, garam masala, roasted crushed peanuts and salt to taste. Mix until all the ingredients are well combined.

- Divide the mixture into 8 portions and flatten them into thick discs.

- Place the tikkis on a preheated pan, drizzle a little oil over each tikki. Cook on both sides until golden.

- Once done, remove from heat and transfer to a serving bowl. After it cools, pack into the lunch box.

Creamy Tomato Pasta, Stir-Fried Zucchini, Khakhra, Quick Home-made Yogurt Dessert (p 41)

Spinach Corn Quesadilla, Grapes (p 35)

Mushroom Biryani, Raita, Papad (p 98)

Green Moong Dal Pulao, Raita, Energy Bar, Makhana (p 101)

Matar Paneer, Kala Channa Salad, Paratha (p 125)

Methi Bajra Thepla, Channa Masala, Buttermilk (p 111)

Palak Paneer Roll, Guava (p 73)

Beetroot Rice, Stir-Fried Broccoli, Watermelon Juice (p 95)

Carrot Corn Mayo Sandwich, Fruits (p 19)

Dal Makhani, Jeera Aloo Sabzi, Jeera Rice, Fruits, Nuts (p 103)

Mixed Rice Ideas

Mixed Rice Ideas

34

Vegetable Tomato Rice (Thakkali Sadam) and Curd

With a burst of flavours in every bite, this tangy Vegetable Tomato Rice is a perfectly balanced delight for young taste buds. Pair it with the cool creaminess of curd for a winning combination.

Tip: Use cooked rice from the previous day, and it will be a breeze to put the lunch box together.

Makes: 4 servings

Ingredients

- 2 tbsp sesame oil
- 1 tsp cumin seeds
- ½ tsp mustard seeds
- 10 pearl onions (sambar onions), finely chopped
- 1-inch ginger, finely chopped
- 4 cloves garlic, finely chopped
- 3 tomatoes, finely chopped

2 carrots, grated (optional)
1 sprig curry leaves, finely chopped
1 tsp sambar powder
½ tsp turmeric powder
1 tsp cardamom powder
6 sprigs mint leaves, finely chopped
1 cup cooked rice
Salt to taste
1 tbsp ghee

Method

- Heat sesame oil in a heavy-bottomed pan over medium heat. Add cumin seeds and mustard seeds; allow them to crackle. Then add onions, ginger and garlic, and sauté until the onions are tender and golden.

- Add the tomatoes and carrots, and sauté until they are tender and the moisture has evaporated.

- Continue to cook until the mixture looks like a semi-thick paste. Stir in the curry leaves.

- Next, add the sambar powder, turmeric powder, cardamom powder and salt, and mix well.

- Add mint leaves and sauté for a few more minutes. Gradually stir the cooked rice into the tomato mixture and fold the Thakkali Sadam gently so that all ingredients are well combined.

- Finally, add 1 tbsp of ghee and stir it into the Thakkali Sadam. Let the rice cool and pack it in the lunch box along with curd or papad.

35

Cabbage Rice, Stir-Fried Vegetables, Raita

This simple yet delicious Cabbage Rice is a perfect blend of veggies and rice that is as flavourful as it is nutritious. Optionally, pack it along with Stir-Fried Vegetables and Raita (Page 80). This trio is designed to keep young minds and bodies fuelled for the day ahead. With every bite, kids get a balanced and tasty experience, making lunchtime both exciting and wholesome.

Tip: Freezing the curd or the raita the previous night will prevent it from turning sour.

Makes: 4 servings

Ingredients

- 1 tbsp oil
- ½ tsp cumin seeds
- 1 tsp white urad dal (split)
- 1 onion, thinly sliced

2 green chillies, finely chopped or slit
1-inch ginger, finely chopped
2 cups cabbage, thinly sliced/shredded
½ tsp turmeric powder
1 cup cooked rice
Small bunch of coriander leaves, finely chopped
1 tbsp ghee
Salt to taste

Method

- Heat oil in a heavy-bottomed pan over medium heat. Add the cumin seeds and urad dal; allow the cumin seeds to crackle and the dal to turn golden brown and crisp.
- Add the onion, green chillies and ginger, and sauté until the onion is tender and softened. Add the cabbage; sprinkle a little salt and turmeric powder and stir to combine. Cover the pan until the cabbage is soft, tender and cooked.
- Stir in the cooked rice, coriander leaves, salt and ghee, and simmer for a couple of more minutes to infuse the rice with all the flavours. Check the salt and adjust the taste. Turn off the heat.
- Allow the rice to cool and pack into the lunch box with Raita or plain curd and optionally with Stir-Fried Vegetables.

Stir-Fried Vegetables

You can choose a mix of carrots and beans or broccoli. Add a little oil in the pan, toss in the cumins seeds and allow them to crackle, add the cut veggies, sprinkle salt and stir-fry until cooked. Sprinkle a little black pepper powder and pack.

36

Lemon Rice, Curd, Stir-Fried Broccoli

This is a zestful lunch box packed with the tangy goodness of Lemon Rice paired with creamy curd for a cool contrast and a side of Stir-Fried Broccoli for a healthy crunch. This trio creates a meal that is not only delicious but also packed with essential nutrients.

Tip: Ensure you have some cooked rice ready. Using rice that is a day old helps as the grains will be well-separated.

Makes: 4 servings

Ingredients

- 1 tbsp sesame oil
- 1 tsp mustard seeds
- 1 tsp white urad dal (split)
- ¼ cup raw peanuts
- 1 sprig curry leaves, roughly chopped
- 1-inch ginger, grated
- 2 green chillies, finely chopped

1 tsp turmeric powder
1 cup cooked rice (with well-separated grains)
1 tbsp lemon juice
Salt to taste
Small bunch of coriander leaves, finely chopped

Method

- Heat oil in a heavy-bottomed pan over low heat. Add the mustard seeds, the urad dal and peanuts. Allow the mustard seeds to crackle and roast the dal and peanuts well. The dal should be golden brown and the peanuts crisp. Do this on low heat so that the peanuts get roasted evenly.

- Next, add the curry leaves, ginger, green chillies and turmeric, and stir for a few seconds.

- Add the cooked rice, sprinkle some salt and give it a good stir so that all the ingredients are combined well and the rice is well coated. Cover the pan and allow the Lemon Rice to steam along with the seasoning for a couple of minutes.

- Squeeze the lemon over the rice and stir so that the juice is incorporated evenly. Check the salt and spice levels and adjust to suit your taste. Turn off the heat and stir in the chopped coriander leaves. Once cooled, pack into the lunch box.

Stir-Fried Broccoli

Add a little oil into the pan, toss in the cumin seeds and allow them to crackle, add the cut broccoli florets, sprinkle salt and stir-fry until cooked. Sprinkle a little black pepper powder. Once cooled, pack into the lunch box.

37

Beetroot Rice, Stir-Fried Broccoli, Watermelon Juice

With the vibrant colours of the Beetroot Rice and the crunchy bites of the Stir-Fried Broccoli (Page 94), this makes for a wholesome and appealing meal. Pack with a Watermelon Juice when in season for a hydrating and naturally sweet treat for your child.

Tip: Keep the cooked rice ready the previous day, as it makes the morning prep much quicker.

Makes: 4 servings

Ingredients

- 1 tsp oil
- ½ tsp mustard seeds
- ½ tsp cumin seeds
- 1 sprig curry leaves, finely chopped

1-inch ginger, finely chopped
1 onion, finely chopped
2 tomatoes, finely chopped
½ tsp turmeric powder
1 tsp sambar powder
2 beetroots, finely grated
1 tsp cardamom powder
1 cup cooked rice (with well-separated grains)
1 tbsp ghee
Small bunch of coriander leaves, finely chopped
Salt to taste

Method

- Heat the oil in a wok. Add the mustard seeds and cumin seeds and allow them to crackle. Next, add the curry leaves, ginger and onion. Sauté the onion until tender.
- Add the tomatoes, turmeric and sambar powder, and give a stir. Let it cook for about 1 to 2 minutes until the tomatoes turn soft.
- Next, add the beetroot and salt, and stir to combine well.
- At this stage, turn the heat to low and cover the pan. Simmer for about 4 to 5 minutes until the beetroot softens. Taste it to see if you like the cooked texture, else cook it for a little longer till it is softer.
- Once the beetroot is cooked, add the cardamom powder and cooked rice, and stir to combine. Add the ghee and the coriander leaves.

- Check the salt and spice levels at this stage and adjust to suit your taste.
- Once all the ingredients are combined well, turn off the heat and the Beetroot Rice is ready. Allow it to cool and pack into the lunch box.

38

Mushroom Biryani, Raita, Papad

Kids will simply love this Mushroom Biryani that is rich in nutrients as well as flavour. Pack this along with a simple Raita (Page 80) and, for extra crunch, add a crispy Papad that brings a touch of fun to every bite.

Tip: Cooking the biryani the previous day will save you a lot of time and also enhance the flavours of the rice.

Makes: 4 servings

Ingredients

- 2 cups basmati rice
- 1 tbsp oil
- 1-inch cinnamon stick
- 4 cardamom pods
- 3 cloves
- 1 bay leaf, torn into halves

2 onions, thinly sliced
2-inch ginger, finely chopped
6 cloves garlic, finely chopped
3 green chillies, slit
2 tomatoes, finely chopped
1 tsp red chilli powder
¼ tsp turmeric powder
1 tsp coriander powder
1 tsp garam masala powder
2 cups button mushrooms, cut into half
1 cup coconut milk
Small bunch of coriander leaves, finely chopped
1 tbsp ghee
Salt to taste

Method

- Wash the rice and soak it in water for at least 15 minutes.
- Heat oil in a heavy-bottomed pan over medium heat. Add the whole spices: cinnamon, cardamom, cloves and bay leaf.
- Add the onions, ginger, garlic and green chillies and stir well until the onions soften and are lightly browned.
- Add the tomatoes and sprinkle some salt; cook until mushy.
- Add the red chilli powder, turmeric powder, coriander powder and garam masala and mix well. Add the mushrooms and stir for 3 minutes or until they shrink slightly.
- Add 3 cups of water and the coconut milk. Once it starts boiling, drain the water from the soaked rice and add the rice to the pan.

- Cover and cook on medium heat until all the water is absorbed from the rice and it looks fluffy. Turn off the heat and allow the biryani to rest for 5 minutes before stirring.

- Finally, add the coriander leaves, ghee and gently stir the biryani. Allow it to cool and pack into the lunch box.

39

Green Moong Dal Pulao, Raita, Energy Bar, Makhana

For a mid-morning meal, let the child enjoy the goodness of roasted makhana and an energy bar (Page 63)—light and crunchy, they make for the perfect munch. This combo is designed to keep young minds and bodies fuelled. For lunch, go for a wholesome Green Moong Dal Pulao brimming with protein and taste, and pack it with a Raita (Page 80). This power-packed lunch is all about energy-inducing tasty bites for a hectic school day.

Tip: Cooking this pulao the previous day will save you a lot of time in the morning.

Makes: 4 servings

Ingredients

- 1 tbsp ghee
- ½ tsp cumin seeds
- 1-inch cinnamon stick

2 cardamom pods
1 onion, finely chopped
1-inch ginger, finely chopped
4 cloves garlic, finely chopped
2 green chillies, slit
2 tomatoes, finely chopped
½ tsp turmeric powder
1 cup rice, washed and soaked in 2 cups of water for 1 hour and drained
1 cup green moong dal, soaked for 5 to 6 hours or overnight
½ cup beans, finely chopped
2 carrots, finely chopped
Salt to taste
Small bunch of coriander leaves, finely chopped

Method

- Heat ghee in a pressure cooker on medium heat. Add the cumin seeds and allow them to crackle. Add the cinnamon and cardamom, allowing them to release their aroma.

- Stir in the onion, ginger, garlic and green chillies, and sauté on medium heat until the onion turns translucent and soft and begins to give off a sweet smell.

- Stir in the tomatoes and turmeric powder. Sauté until the tomatoes are cooked through. Stir in the rice, green moong dal, beans, carrots and salt along with 2½ cups of water.

- Cover the pressure cooker and cook the Green Dal Moong Pulao for 3 to 4 whistles and turn off the heat. Allow the pressure to release naturally.

- Open the pressure cooker, stir in the coriander leaves. Transfer the Green Moong Dal Pulao to a bowl. For the lunch box, allow the rice to cool before packing.

40

Dal Makhani, Jeera Aloo Sabzi, Jeera Rice, Fruits, Nuts

With this meal, kids will have nothing short of a feast with friends. This creamy Dal Makhani, paired with Jeera Aloo Sabzi and Jeera Rice (Page 83), is a wholesome meal. And there's more—a burst of sweetness with fresh fruits and a crunch of nuts for energy.

Tip: I often make these dishes for dinner and simply keep aside some of it for packing into the lunch box the next day. If made the previous evening, simply warm it a little before packing for lunch. Alternatively, you can also simply pack the Dal Makhani with Phulka for lunch along with the fruits and nuts.

Makes: 4 servings

Ingredients

  2 tbsp ghee
  1 tsp cumin seeds
  1-inch ginger, finely chopped
  4 cloves garlic, finely chopped

2 green chillies, finely chopped
1 bay leaf, torn
1-inch cinnamon stick, broken
3 cardamom pods
1 tomato, finely chopped
¼ tsp turmeric powder
½ tsp cumin powder
½ tsp garam masala powder
1 tsp Kashmiri red chilli powder
¾ cup whole black urad dal, soaked for 8 hours or overnight
¼ cup fresh cream
1 tbsp kasuri methi
Salt to taste

Method

- Heat ghee in a pressure cooker over medium heat. Add the cumin seeds and allow them to crackle. Add the ginger, garlic and green chillies and sauté for a few seconds.
- Add the bay leaf, cinnamon, cardamom, tomato, turmeric, cumin powder, garam masala powder and red chilli powder. Sauté on medium heat until the tomato softens.
- Add the soaked dal along with more water until the dal mixture has at least 2 inches of water above it. Add salt to taste and cover the pressure cooker.
- Pressure cook for about 35 to 40 minutes on medium heat, then turn off the heat and allow the pressure to release naturally.
- When you open the cooker, the dal should be well-cooked. Add water to get the right consistency if it has become a little thick.
- Stir in the cream and kasuri methi. Bring to a simmer and keep mashing the dal to make it creamy. This will also help deepen the flavours.

- Traditionally, dals are simmered for more than an hour or two to draw out the intense richness and taste. But make sure that when you simmer the dal, it is stirred occasionally so that it does not stick to the bottom of the pan.
- Turn off the heat. Pack into the lunch box when cool.

Jeera Aloo Sabzi

Makes: 4 servings

Ingredients

1 tbsp oil
1 tbsp cumin seeds
½ tsp asafoetida
3 potatoes, peeled and cut into wedges
½ tsp red chilli powder
½ tsp turmeric powder
½ tsp coriander powder
½ tsp dry mango (amchur) powder
Salt to taste
Small bunch of coriander leaves, finely chopped

Method

- Heat oil in a wide pan over medium heat. Add cumin seeds and asafoetida. Once the cumin seeds crackle, add the potatoes and all the remaining ingredients. Toss well to combine.
- Cover the pan and allow the potatoes to cook on low to medium heat until cooked through completely.
- Turn off the heat and garnish with coriander leaves. Allow it to cool a bit before packing into the lunch box.

Roti Sabzi Ideas

41

Broccoli Aloo Sabzi, Phulka, Fruit Salad

Here is an absolute feast with a Broccoli Aloo Sabzi, a medley of veggies that is both flavourful and nutritious. Serve it with soft Phulkas and add a vibrant fruit salad or simply cut some seasonal fruits for a refreshing touch. Kids will get the energy they need to conquer the school day with enthusiasm.

Tip: Phulkas can be made the previous evening to free up time in the morning.

Makes: 4 servings

Ingredients

- ½ tsp mustard seeds
- 3 potatoes, peeled and cut into wedges
- ½ tsp turmeric powder
- 1 tsp red chilli powder
- 1 broccoli, cut into florets

1 sprig curry leaves, roughly torn
Salt to taste
Oil, for cooking

Note: The broccoli and potatoes will be cooked separately as the cooking time differs for both vegetables.

Method

- Heat 1 tsp oil in a kadai. Add the mustard seeds and allow them to crackle. Add the potato wedges, curry leaves, sprinkle salt and stir-fry until cooked through. Cover the pan while the potatoes are cooking as the steam created will make them cook faster.

- Add the turmeric powder and red chilli powder. Sauté till the spices coat the potatoes. Once done, turn off the heat, transfer the potatoes to a dish and keep aside.

- In the same kadai, heat ½ tsp oil and add the broccoli florets. Sprinkle some salt and stir-fry until the broccoli is just about cooked through. Cover the pan while cooking as the steam created makes the broccoli cook faster.

- Once the broccoli is cooked, stir in the roasted potatoes. Check the salt and spices, adjust to suit your taste. Allow it to cool before you pack into the lunch box.

42

Methi Bajra Thepla, Channa Masala, Buttermilk

This is a lunch box with the wholesome goodness of Methi Bajra Thepla along with protein-rich Channa Masala and, for a refreshing touch, there's cool and soothing Buttermilk. This is a complete meal that combines taste and health—perfect for growing minds.

Tip: Keep the Channa Masala and the dough for the Methi Bajra Thepla ready the previous day. Instead of Buttermilk, you can even pack plain curd.

Methi Bajra Thepla

Makes: 10–12 theplas
Ingredients

    1 cup bajra flour
    1 cup wholewheat flour
    ½ tsp turmeric powder

½ tsp black pepper powder
1 tsp salt
1-inch ginger, grated
1 green chilli, finely chopped
½ cup methi leaves, finely chopped
Oil, for cooking

Method

- Combine the bajra flour, wholewheat flour, turmeric powder, black pepper powder, ginger, green chilli and methi leaves in a large mixing bowl.
- Add water, a little at a time, and knead to make a smooth and firm dough. Drizzle some oil on top and knead for a few more minutes until smooth. Cover the thepla dough and allow it to rest for 30 minutes.
- Preheat an iron skillet on medium heat. Divide the dough into 10–12 portions.
- Roll the thepla portions into balls and flatten them with the palm of your hand. Toss the thepla dough portions on flour and roll them out into thin circles that are approximately 6 inches in diameter.
- As you roll them out, you can keep tossing them in dry flour to prevent them from sticking.
- Follow the same process with the remaining balls. Ideally, you should roll out all portions of the dough before you start cooking them.
- With the skillet on high heat, place a rolled-out thepla on the skillet. After a few seconds, you will notice small air pockets forming.

- At this point, flip the thepla and smear ½ tsp oil on it. Now, using a flat spatula, do a light pressing-and-turning motion to cook the thepla.
- Flip the thepla and use the same press-and-turn method for the other side. You will notice brown spots all over the cooked thepla. Remove from heat and place it on a flat plate.
- Repeat this process with the remaining rolled-out portions and stack the cooked theplas one on top of the other. Stacking them maintains their softness and retains moisture, preventing them from drying out.

Channa Masala

Makes: 4 servings

Ingredients

1 cup Kabuli channa, soaked for 8 hours or overnight
1 tsp oil
1 tsp cumin seeds
1 onion, thinly sliced
1-inch ginger, finely chopped
1 bay leaf
1 tomato, finely chopped
½ tsp turmeric powder
1 tbsp dry mango (amchur) powder
1 tbsp garam masala powder
1 tsp pomegranate seed (anardana) powder
1 tsp coriander powder
½ tsp red chilli powder
½ tsp black pepper powder
1 tsp black salt

Salt to taste
Small bunch of coriander leaves, finely chopped

Method

- Pressure cook the soaked channa with salt, using the water in which it was soaked (add more if required) for 35 to 40 minutes until the channa is soft and tender. You will know it is cooked perfectly when you can mash the channa easily between your fingers. Keep the cooked channa aside.

- Heat oil in a large, heavy-bottomed pan. Add the cumin seeds and allow them to crackle. Add the onion, ginger and bay leaf, and stir-fry until the onion becomes soft and translucent.

- Stir in the tomato, turmeric powder, dry mango powder, garam masala, pomegranate seed powder, coriander powder, red chilli powder, black pepper powder and black salt. Sauté until the tomato softens.

- Next, add the cooked channa into the masala. Stir well so that the channa is coated with the masala. Check the salt and spice levels and adjust to suit your taste. Cover the pan, turn the heat to low and simmer for 20 to 30 minutes. Give the masala a final taste check and stir in the chopped coriander leaves.

43

Palak Paratha, Chhole Tamatari

This combo of a vibrant green Palak Paratha and Chhole Tamatari—protein-packed chickpeas in a tomato gravy, offering a burst of tangy flavours—brings both taste and health to the table. It makes lunchtime exciting and wholesome, fuelling the kids for a day of learning.

Tip: Prepare the paratha dough and cook the Chhole Tamatari the previous day.

Palak Paratha

Makes: 6 to 8 parathas

Ingredients

    200 gm spinach, finely chopped
    2 green chillies, finely chopped
    2 cups wholewheat flour

1 tsp fennel seeds, roasted and coarsely pounded
1 tsp turmeric powder
1 tsp cumin powder
Salt to taste
1 tbsp oil
Ghee, for cooking

Method

- Heat 1 tsp ghee in a pan over medium heat. Add the spinach and allow it to soften. Turn off the heat and let the spinach cool completely.
- In a large bowl, combine all the ingredients, including the cooked spinach, and knead, adding a little water at a time to make a firm and smooth dough. Add 1 tbsp oil to coat the dough and knead again.
- Divide the dough into 8 portions. Preheat an iron skillet on medium heat.
- Roll the dough portions into balls and flatten them with the palm of your hand. Toss them in flour and roll them out into circles that are approximately 3 inches in diameter.
- We need to make a triangular shape for the parathas. For this, first fold the rolled-out circle into a semicircle, then fold the semicircle in half to get a mini triangle. Tossing the triangle in a little flour, roll it out gently into a big triangle. Repeat the process for the remaining dough portions.
- Place one rolled-out Palak Paratha on a skillet on medium-high heat. After a few seconds, you will notice air pockets forming. At this point, flip the Palak Paratha and spread about ½ tsp ghee on it. Using a flat spatula, do a light pressing-and-turning motion to cook the paratha.

- Flip the paratha and repeat the process. You will notice brown spots on the paratha and it will be slightly crisp. Remove from heat and place on a platter. Pack into the lunch box after it cools.

Chhole Tamatari

Makes: 4 servings

Ingredients

1 cup Kabuli channa, soaked for 8 to 10 hours
1 tbsp oil
1 onion, finely chopped
1-inch ginger, finely chopped
2 cloves garlic, finely chopped
3 tomatoes, puréed
½ tsp turmeric powder
1 tsp coriander powder
1 tsp garam masala powder
1 tsp red chilli powder
1-inch cinnamon stick
2 cardamom pods
1 bay leaf, torn
Salt to taste
Small bunch of coriander leaves, finely chopped

Method

- Pressure cook the channa with salt, using the water in which it was soaked (add more if required) for 35 to 40 minutes, until it is soft and tender. You will know it is cooked perfectly when you can mash the channa easily between your fingers. Keep the cooked channa aside.

- Heat oil in a pan over medium heat. Add the onion, ginger and garlic, and sauté until the onion becomes soft and translucent.
- Stir in the tomato purée, turmeric powder, coriander powder, garam masala powder, red chilli powder, cardamom pods, cinnamon stick, bay leaves and salt. Cook the mixture until the tomato and onion are well cooked and there is no raw smell. The mixture will thicken and come together.
- Add the cooked channa, with a little more water if required. Stir to combine. Allow the mixture to simmer over medium heat for 15 to 20 minutes.
- Adjust the consistency, stir in the coriander leaves and adjust seasoning of the dish according to your taste. Once done, turn off the heat, allow it to cool and pack into the lunchbox.

Desi Masala Pasta, Banana, Boiled Eggs (p 39)

Grilled Tomato Cheese Pesto Sandwich, Guava, Almonds, Apricots (p 25)

Aloo Paratha, Pomegranate, Raita (p 78)

Mushroom Quesadilla, Walnuts, Raisins (p 37)

Cabbage Rice, Stir-Fried Vegetables, Raita (p 91)

Paneer Makhani, Pudina Paratha, Raita (p 120)

Broccoli Aloo Sabzi, Phulka, Fruit Salad, Cookies (p 107)

Cucumber Cheese Sandwich, Walnuts, Banana Almond Date Shake, Muffin (p 21)

Moong Dal Podi Idli, Chutney, Watermelon (p 55)

Bagel Pizza and Cookies (p 27)

44

Paneer Makhani, Pudina Paratha, Raita

Kids will absolutely love the all-time classics Paneer Makhani, Pudina Paratha and Raita (Page 80) when packed into a lunch box. This will bring a delicious excitement to lunchtime, while also offering a balanced and delightful meal.

Paneer Makhani

Makes: 4 servings

Ingredients

- 1 onion, roughly chopped
- 1-inch ginger
- 4 cloves garlic
- 1 tsp turmeric powder
- ½ tsp cumin powder
- ½ tsp red chilli powder
- 1 tsp cardamom powder

½ tsp garam masala powder
2 cups home-made tomato purée
¼ cup fresh cream
2 tsp honey
1 tbsp kasuri methi
250 gm paneer, cut into cubes
Salt to taste
Oil, for cooking

Method

- Make a smooth paste of the onion, ginger and garlic in a mixer-grinder.
- Heat oil in a heavy-bottomed pan over medium heat. Add the onion mixture and sauté on medium heat until it loses its raw smell. This will take about 4 minutes approximately.
- Next, add the turmeric powder, cumin powder, red chilli powder, cardamom powder and garam masala powder, and stir-fry it along with the onion paste for about 2 minutes. This process of sautéing the masala helps the onion lose its raw smell faster.
- When the mixture is well sautéed, add the tomato purée and simmer until it begins to bubble and boil.
- Stir in the cream, honey, salt, kasuri methi and paneer. Give the Paneer Makhani a good stir and simmer for another 3 to 4 minutes.
- Check the salt and spice levels and adjust to suit your taste. Turn off the heat and transfer the Paneer Makhani to a serving bowl. Allow it to cool and pack into the lunch box.

Pudina Paratha

Makes: 6 to 8 parathas

Ingredients

    100 gm pudina leaves, finely chopped
    2 green chillies, finely chopped
    2 cups wholewheat flour
    ½ tsp turmeric powder
    ½ tsp cumin powder
    ½ tsp red chilli powder
    1 tbsp oil
    Salt to taste
    Ghee, for cooking

Method

- In a large bowl, combine all the ingredients, including the chopped pudina, and knead, adding a little water at a time to make a firm and smooth dough. Add 1 tbsp oil to coat the dough and knead again.
- Divide the dough into 8 portions. Preheat an iron skillet on medium heat.
- Roll the dough portions into balls and flatten them with the palm of your hand. Toss them in flour and roll them out into circles that are approximately 3 inches in diameter.
- We need to make a triangular shape for the parathas. For this, first fold the rolled-out circle into a semicircle, then fold the semicircle in half to get a mini triangle. Tossing the triangle in a little flour, roll it out gently into a big triangle. Repeat the process for the remaining dough portions.

- On medium-high heat, place one rolled-out Pudina Paratha on the skillet. After a few seconds, you will notice air pockets forming. Flip the paratha and smear about ½ tsp ghee on it. Using a flat spatula, do a light pressing-and-turning motion to cook the paratha.
- Flip the paratha to cook the other side in the same way, using the press-and-turn motion. You will notice brown spots on the paratha and it will be slightly crisp.
- Remove from heat and place on a platter. Pack into the lunch box once it cools.

45

Quick Gobi Sabzi, Tawa Paratha

Dive into Quick Gobi Sabzi where cauliflower florets are cooked to perfection in a medley of spices. Pack it along with soft Tawa Parathas for a burst of taste and nutrition. Add some fresh fruits, curd or even buttermilk in a leak-proof bottle for a refreshing finish.

Makes: 4 servings

Ingredients

- 1 tbsp oil
- ½ tsp cumin seeds
- 1 onion, finely chopped
- 1-inch ginger, finely chopped
- 4 cloves garlic, finely chopped
- 1 cauliflower, cut into florets
- 3 tomatoes, finely chopped
- 1 tsp turmeric powder
- ½ tsp red chilli powder
- 1 tsp garam masala powder

Small bunch of coriander leaves, finely chopped
Salt to taste

Method

- Heat oil in a heavy-bottomed pan over medium heat. Add the cumin seeds and allow them to crackle. Add the onion, ginger and garlic, and allow the onion to soften and turn translucent.
- Add the cauliflower with some salt and steam until partially cooked. Halfway through the cooking process, add the chopped tomatoes, turmeric powder, red chilli powder and garam masala powder. Cover the pan and cook until the tomatoes have softened and the cauliflower is cooked through.
- Stir occasionally so the spices are well combined. Once done, check the salt and spice levels and adjust to suit your taste, then turn off the heat. Stir in the chopped coriander leaves and pack into the lunchbox.

Tawa Paratha

You can make a Pudina Paratha (Page 121) or simply skip the pudina and chillies and make a plain paratha for packing into the lunch box.

46

Matar Paneer, Kala Channa Salad, Paratha

This is a delicious lunch starring Matar Paneer and a Kala Channa Salad that works well as a snack too. Your kid's day is set with a protein-packed meal designed to fuel both learning and play.

Tip: Prepare the salad for the snack box and keep the dough for the paratha ready the previous evening. Try a paratha similar to Pudina Paratha (Page 121).

Matar Paneer

Makes: 4 servings

Ingredients

- 1 tbsp ghee
- 2 cloves
- 2 brown cardamoms (badi elaichi)
- 1 tsp black peppercorns, coarsely pounded

1 onion, finely chopped
1-inch ginger, finely chopped
4 cloves garlic, finely chopped
¼ tsp turmeric powder
½ tsp red chilli powder
¼ tsp coriander powder
¼ tsp cumin powder
½ tsp garam masala powder
5 tomatoes, cut and puréed
1 tsp sugar
1 tsp kasuri methi
250 gm paneer, cut into cubes
1 tbsp butter
½ cup frozen green peas, thawed
Salt to taste
Small bunch of coriander leaves, finely chopped

Method

- Heat ghee in a pan over medium heat. Add the cloves, cardamom and pepper. Stir-fry for a few seconds till they release their aroma.
- Add the onion, ginger and garlic, and sauté until the onion becomes soft and tender.
- Add the turmeric powder, red chilli powder, coriander powder, cumin powder and garam masala powder and give it a stir.
- Add the tomato purée, salt and sugar and give the mixture a stir. Allow the tomato masala to come to a brisk boil. Next, stir in the kasuri methi, paneer, butter and thawed green peas.
- Cover the pan and let the Matar Paneer simmer for about 5 minutes. Turn off the heat, and taste for salt and spice levels.

Finally, stir in the coriander leaves. Pack the Matar Paneer into the lunch box.

Kala Channa Salad

Makes: 4 servings

Ingredients

2 cups kala channa, soaked for 8 hours or overnight
1 onion, finely chopped
1 tomato, finely chopped
2 green chillies, finely chopped
1 tsp lemon juice
½ tsp chaat masala
Salt to taste
Small bunch of coriander leaves, finely chopped

Method

- Pressure cook the channa using the water in which it was soaked for 30 minutes until well cooked.
- Allow the pressure to release naturally. Drain the water; transfer the kala channa to a bowl and set aside.
- In a mixing bowl, combine the boiled kala channa, onion, tomato, green chillies, salt, lemon juice, chaat masala and coriander leaves. Mix well and pack into the lunch box.

47

Palak Paneer, Tawa Paratha, Cucumber Salad

Kids will simply love indulging in this delightful Palak Paneer and Tawa Paratha (Page 124) combo, with a side of Cucumber Salad that adds a pop of freshness. This trio brings together taste, nutrition and fun, making lunchtime an enjoyable experience.

Makes: 4 servings

Ingredients

- 1 tbsp ghee
- 1-inch ginger, finely chopped
- 2 cloves garlic, finely chopped
- 1 tomato, chopped
- 2 green chillies, slit
- ½ tsp cumin powder
- 1 tsp garam masala powder
- 1-inch cinnamon stick

500 gm spinach, chopped
1 tbsp butter
1 tsp cumin seeds
2 tbsp fresh cream
200 gm paneer, cut into cubes
Salt to taste

Method

- Heat ghee in a pressure cooker over medium heat. Add the ginger, garlic, tomato, green chillies, cumin powder, garam masala powder and cinnamon. Sauté for a few minutes until the tomato turns slightly soft.
- Add the chopped spinach and salt. Give it a stir and add 1 tbsp water.
- Cover the pressure cooker and cook the spinach for just one whistle. Turn off the heat and release the pressure immediately by using a fork and lifting the weight or by placing the cooker under cold running water. We release the pressure immediately in order to retain the fresh green colour of the spinach. Open the cooker and allow the spinach to cool completely.
- Pulse the spinach in the blender to make a smooth purée. You can also choose to blend the spinach with a masher to give it a different texture.
- Melt the butter in a frying pan on medium heat. Add cumin seeds and allow them to crackle.
- Next, stir in the palak purée, cream and paneer. Check the salt and adjust according to taste.
- Give the Palak Paneer a brisk boil for 3 to 4 minutes and turn off the heat. Transfer the Palak Paneer to the lunch box.

Acknowledgements

A big thank you to the fans of Archana's Kitchen who constantly keep trying out and requesting recipes across cuisines for kids' lunch boxes, meal plans and even special diets for those with diabetes, cholesterol and so on.

My boys, Siddhant and Pranav, for whom all these school lunch boxes were packed every single day and who would ensure they brought them back home empty. Well, on most days at least. They are my biggest critics who would smell the food being cooked from their rooms, know the aromas of the spices being added and eat everything I would place on their plates. I hope they will find my recipes useful as they venture into their own kitchens and pack their kids' lunch boxes.

My lovely editor, Trisha, and the team at HarperCollins India who worked as hard as me to bring this book to life. Thank you.

About the Author

Archana Doshi is an entrepreneur, food activist, wife and mother. In 2007, she founded Archana's Kitchen which soon grew into India's leading food and recipe platform. Over two decades later, Archana's Kitchen has over 10 million users across multiple platforms, including her website, YouTube channel, social media pages and mobile app. She was featured as a 'Google Entrepreneur on the Web' for her outstanding work on food in the digital space and was the inspiration for the first Google Chrome Ad on national television in India. She is passionate about teaching people the basics of home cooking and the nutritional aspects of simple Indian meals.

Visit her website: https://www.archanaskitchen.com/

YouTube channel: https://www.youtube.com/channel/UCFaHKVsssaoZxM4WZLU0pCA

HarperCollins *Publishers* India

At HarperCollins India, we believe in telling the best stories and finding the widest readership for our books in every format possible. We started publishing in 1992; a great deal has changed since then, but what has remained constant is the passion with which our authors write their books, the love with which readers receive them, and the sheer joy and excitement that we as publishers feel in being a part of the publishing process.

Over the years, we've had the pleasure of publishing some of the finest writing from the subcontinent and around the world, including several award-winning titles and some of the biggest bestsellers in India's publishing history. But nothing has meant more to us than the fact that millions of people have read the books we published, and that somewhere, a book of ours might have made a difference.

As we look to the future, we go back to that one word— a word which has been a driving force for us all these years.

Read.